(Front cover) Hunter of Central Australia.

(Left) A man from southeast Australia, near Adelaide, posing for an early photograph, probably in the 1860s.

(Right) Australia. Heaviest shading indicates highest rain.

INDONESIA

NEW GUI

Melville I

Arnhem Land

Cape York

NORTHERN TERRITORY

Kimberley

QUEENSLAND

DESERT

WESTERN AUSTRALIA

Adelaide

NEW SOUTH WALES

VICTORIA

SOUTH AUSTRALIA

TASMANIA

When the British first began to settle in Australia, from 1788 onwards, it was a land of natural vegetation and wildlife which seemed hardly touched by human habitation, even though the Aborigines had been living there for perhaps as long as 60,000 years. The Aborigines lived entirely from the wild produce of the land, a way of life which the Europeans inevitably destroyed when they took the land for their own use. Until this time the Aborigines had known very little contact with the rest of the world, and they developed a distinctive culture of their own. On the northern coasts the people of Arnhem Land had been visited by Indonesian traders, and there was some contact between Cape York and New Guinea, but these outsiders had little influence on Aboriginal life in general. European settlers were first attracted to the fertile coastal areas of the southeast and southwest of Australia. The settlers soon outnumbered the local Aborigines, for whom this had also been the richest part of the continent, and their traditional way of life was destroyed before anyone cared to make a serious study of it. Most of what is known about Aboriginal life comes from the desert centre

1

and the north of Australia. More recently Europeans have taken posses-
sion of these areas as well, for various purposes from stock raising
to mining and rocket testing.

Living off the land

As farmers, herdsmen and industrialists Europeans in Australia have
changed the environment to suit their needs and they can support a
vastly larger population than that of the Aborigines. Before Europeans
arrived there were probably no more than 300,000 people in the whole
of Australia. This population had probably not increased since earliest
times, and was all that the Aboriginal way of life could comfortably
support. Wild foods are nowhere so abundant in Australia (or most
other parts of the world) that people living on these alone can stay
in one place for any length of time as they can by farming or trade.
The Aborigines moved continually from one place to another as local
foods came into season, revisiting places only after supplies had been
replenished by natural growth.

In the fertile regions food could be found with little trouble, but
even the most arid deserts of central Australia could support Aborigines
living off the land. The desert people had to move on more often,
and cover greater distances, but their life was seldom a desperate struggle
for survival. Vegetable foods gathered by the women formed much
the largest part of the Aboriginal diet. The men might spend hours
or days patiently stalking and tracking wild animals, and still return
empty-handed if they were unlucky. Wild plants were a more reliable
food supply which could be gathered with much less time and labour.

Aborigines travelled light, burdened by few possessions. As they could
always move on to new supplies of food, to be gathered when needed,
they did not usually need to store food for future use or carry it with
them. Their huts or simple shelters of bark or brushwood were built
anew wherever they set up camp. In some areas they built only rough
windbreaks, or slept completely in the open, warming themselves against
the cold desert nights with small fires. In the south and southeast
of Australia fur wraps were worn, but in most areas nothing was worn
but simple ornaments. The tools and equipment needed to gain a living
from the land were few and simple, designed to be useful without being
complicated. People could carry these with them wherever they went.

For women the basic tool was a simple sharpened stick, which was
used for digging up edible roots like wild yams or unearthing small
creatures for food. Soil was loosened with thrusts from the stick and
scooped away by hand. Women also gathered various wild fruits, berries,
nuts, and grass seeds, birds' eggs, large grubs and other edible insects.
They caught small creatures like frogs, lizards and snakes, mice, bandi-
coots and possums for food. For collecting food, among other things,
women used various types of baskets and bags. Depending on what
they were used for, these were plaited, made from string or from sheets

An Arnhem Land man with his spear and spearthrower, carrying a kangaroo he has killed. His metal spearpoint, haircut and loincloth show European influence (1951).

of bark, and they also varied from one region to another. In southern and central Australia large wooden bowls were used, not only for food, but for carrying babies, water and anything else. They were basic all-purpose utensils, and were also used for instance to scoop earth when digging, or to winnow the husks from grass seeds by tossing the seed in the wind *(see inside back cover)*.

On the move a man carried only his weapons, which were used for fighting, but more importantly for hunting, so that he was always ready to attack any game that appeared. Although large animals, such as kangaroos and wallabies, and birds such as emus and cassowaries were the most prized game, all of Australia's wild animals were worth hunting. When animals like rabbits and buffalo were introduced by Europeans these were also hunted. The Australian dog (the dingo) which was the Aborigines' only domestic animal was sometimes used to help with hunting, although it was kept mainly as a pet. Wild dingos might also be killed for food.

A man's basic weapons were his spears. They were made from thin saplings, sharpened at the ends or headed with stone or hardwood points. They were used with a spear-thrower, a stick or board with a peg at one end to fit the butt of the spear. Held at the other end, this acted like an extension of the arm, increasing the force and range of the throw. The people living on the coasts and rivers also used special fishing spears. Throwing sticks (including 'boomerangs') were also important weapons in many areas. They were of various local types, but usually flat and sharp edged. Although simple they were carefully and precisely made, besides being ornamented with carved fluting, painted patterns or engravings. When thrown they spun as they flew and could break bones or inflict gashes, bringing down flying birds or running animals. Boomerangs which returned to the thrower were only used in certain areas, for displays of skill and not as weapons. For fighting men also used various clubs, and carried wooden shields to ward off the blows of throwing sticks, spears and clubs. The Aborigines were not a warlike people but their quarrels often came to blows, and might lead to feuds if someone was killed.

Weapons and most tools were made by men, using tools of stone, bone and animal teeth. A small stone axe was a basic woodworking tool. It was sometimes made by doubling a flexible stick around the stone blade and fixing it with vegetable gum to form a handle. Besides woodworking the axe was useful for cutting footholds when climbing trees or for chopping out beehives. Chisels, often sharp stone flakes or teeth fixed with resinous gum to a wooden handle, were used for finer work on wooden objects.

Aboriginal possessions were most elaborate in the fertile coastal areas where people did not have to travel about so much. Shelters were more solid and tools and utensils were rather more complex than in the interior. On the coasts and rivers canoes were used, and nets were made for fishing. The desert people travelling farther and more often, managed with fewer possessions. They kept their equipment to a mini-

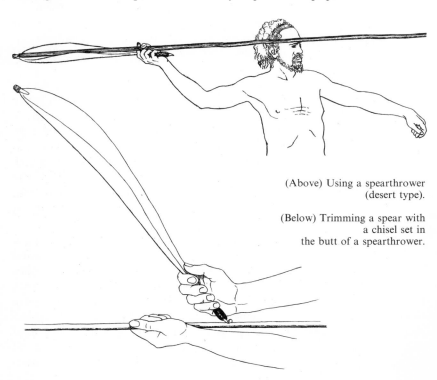

(Above) Using a spearthrower (desert type).

(Below) Trimming a spear with a chisel set in the butt of a spearthrower.

mum by using tools which combined several uses in one object. In some parts the spearthrower also acted as a handle for a chisel blade, which was set into the butt with vegetable resin. These spearthrowers were concave and could also be used as dishes, but in some areas the end of a spearthrower could serve as a digging stick. Some Aborigines carried special fire-making equipment, a hardwood stick which was rotated rapidly between the palms of the hands so that the end drilled into a piece of softwood. The resulting friction produced a smouldering dust to light the fire. Others made fire by rubbing the edge of a hardwood spearthrower back and forth on a softwood shield with the same effect. The recessed handgrip of such a shield might be used to carry water, or the blood used in sacred ceremonies. Throwing sticks could be used as clubs, for digging, or for prising the bark off trees. In short, although Aboriginal tools were few, they had a great many uses.

To gain a living with these simple tools the Aborigines learned remark-able skills and an intimate knowledge of their land. They needed to know the uses of plants, the habits of wild creatures and the seasons and places in which they were to be found. For instance they could tell from a crack in the ground where an edible root such as a wild yam lay buried. Hunters could track wild animals from the faintest signs and even identify the individual footprints of the people they knew. They could approach within spear range of wary animals by creeping silently, freezing on the spot while the creature looked around, until they had the opportunity to strike. In the desert areas knowledge of every waterhole, including even crevices in rocks and trees where rain might collect, was essential to survival.

Community life

An Aboriginal family, a man with one or more wives and their children, could normally provide for itself as far as food was concerned. Usually, though, families travelled and camped in groups or bands. Each day, when the women went out to gather food, and the men perhaps to hunt, everyone would bring most of the food they found back to the camp in the evening. Here the old people and the infirm, who could not help provide food themselves, were provided for, the burden being shared among their relatives.

Families living in the same band were usually related to one another quite closely. These bands were generally quite small, seldom larger than about 30 people, a size which prevented the group consuming all the local food too quickly, and having to move on too often. Families could join or leave a band as they chose, and in bad seasons or years people split up into smaller groups and spread out in search of food. Only when and where food was abundant could large groups of people come together for long periods, and this was usually when they held their big religious festivals. For such occasions all the bands of an area would gather to form a group of several hundred people. These

A woodland camp, probably in coastal New South Wales during the 1860s. The shelters are made of tree bark and brushwood.

people formed a loose-knit community of relatives who only met and lived together from time to time. Such a community, sometimes called a 'tribe' by Europeans, would share the same language and customs, slightly different from those of neighbouring tribes.

Members of Aboriginal communities always regarded themselves as related to one another. As with other peoples who live in small independent communities around the world, family ties were very important in Aboriginal life. People could trace their relatives by blood and marriage in great detail. They did this in a very systematic way, calling distant relatives by the same words as if they were members of their close family. Whether a distant relative was 'father', 'sister', 'cousin' etc, depended on through which individuals the relationship was traced.

The way people were related decided not only which people could not marry one another, but also whom they should marry. Married couples, like everyone else in the community, were relatives, but they had to be related in a particular way. This of course decided who their children should marry, and so on. The community was divided into several sets of people, each set related to the others in such a way that a husband and wife would come from different sets, and their children would belong to yet another. By regulating marriage in this way the Aborigines standardised the ways in which everyone in the community was related to one another. They created perhaps the most complicated pattern of family relationships of any people in the world.

Depending on how people were related they had certain responsibilities to one another, and were expected to treat one another with the proper degree of respect or familiarity. To the Aborigines this was the right and proper way for people to live in society. They regarded European customs as less than human because, like animals, Europeans can marry almost anyone, and do not keep track of their relatives. The Aboriginal system of tracing relationships could be extended indefinitely to include people with whom no actual links were known, according, for instance, to which marriage sets they belonged. Even complete strangers, 'foreigners' speaking different languages, could work out a way of being related to one another so that each knew how they should behave and what they could expect from one another as host or guest.

Belonging to the land and the dreamtime

Groups of people always travelled around within a certain area which they knew intimately. All Aborigines had very strong affection for their own land, feeling that their people had always belonged there, and that each individual belonged to his particular part of the country from birth. The land was more than just their livelihood: they were part of it in a spiritual sense. In the Aborigines' view the people and their land were linked together from the distant past, at the beginning of the world as it is now. At this time the everyday world and the spiritual part of the world, known as the 'dreamtime', were one and the same. In this ancient period sacred beings, the dreamtime people, wandered the earth shaping the landscape, and the places they visited were forever associated with them. Some originated plants and animals and humans, organised Aboriginal society and founded its customs and religious rituals. Throughout much of Australia these beings were thought to be at once both plants or animals and persons. They might be these things in human form; kangaroo-men or wild-yam people for instance. They were also something more than natural creatures or humans, for they had special powers. In some areas particular dreamtime people in human form were most important. Throughout much of eastern and southeastern Australia a hero belonging in the sky was the main dreamtime character. In Arnhem Land and the north certain women from across the sea, and the fabulous 'rainbow serpent', a dreamtime snake, played a large part in the events of the dreamtime. Such achievements were remembered through the Aborigines' sacred tales and chants, and commemorated in their religious rituals.

In many ways the dreamtime people acted like humans and tales about them often described everyday Aboriginal activities–hunting and gathering food, love affairs and family life, quarrels and feuds. However, the things that dreamtime people did were far more significant than the adventures of any ordinary men and women. Their actions had spectacular results, changing into its present form the face of the landscape they travelled over. Rocks might stand for their bodies at places where they lay down to sleep, or paused to scan the countryside; waterholes might mark their camp sites or places where they dug for water. Parts of their bodies might become hills or rocks, their hair grass or bushes, and their tools and implements or scraps of food could be transformed into peculiarly shaped stones or rock formations. At the end of their travels some turned into rocks or went into the ground in waterholes. All such places were sacred because these dreamtime people left some of their spirit there. The plants, animals and people belonging to these places came from the dreamtime people and shared the spiritual presence which was in the land.

The dreamtime people also organised Aboriginal society and invented its customs at the beginning of things. They organised their own relationships by the same complex rules which were later to govern Aboriginal relationships with each other. As the first people to live the Aboriginal way of life, their actions were like a blueprint for the lives of people from then onwards. It was because the dreamtime people lived like this that the Aborigines felt they should do the same. The Aborigines actually trod in the footsteps of the dreamtime people as they travelled the land from one waterhole or hunting ground to another by the same well tested routes. In this way the sacred dreamtime world continued to be part of the way people lived.

The sacred places of the dreamtime in each district were owned by a particular group of men, usually related to one another through their fathers or fathers' fathers and so on. Men belonged to this local 'clan' group because, as individuals they belonged to its land. Each had something of the spirit of a dreamtime person which was deposited in a sacred place in the dreamtime, entering a person at conception or birth. The particular creature, plant or object with which the dreamtime person was identified shared this spirit force. It was the 'totem' of the Aboriginal person or group.

Of course people were often conceived or born far from the country of their fathers, wherever their band was living, and so they often had spirits from places belonging to other clans. They would still belong to their father's clan, and were encouraged to join in the rituals for the dreamtime people of its country. As their 'spirit home' was somewhere else they would also join in the rituals of the clan country where they were conceived or born.

The spirit continued to exist after a person's death. In some places it was believed that the dead went to another land, perhaps over the sea or in the sky, but this spirit, or some part of it, was also said to return to the place from whence it came, in the land. In any case it was reunited with the people of the dreamtime. Some Aborigines believed the spirit could then be reincarnated: for some each person was the reincarnation of a particular dreamtime person. People felt very strongly that they belonged to the place where their spirit came from. Old men especially were keen to live their last days in their own country, to which they would go when they died.

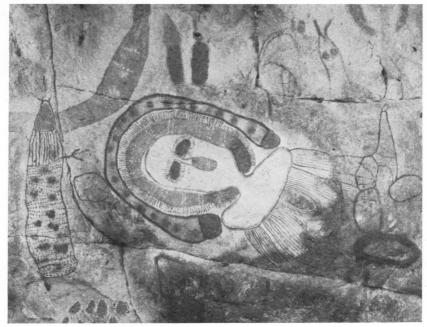

Dreamtime person of the Kimberley area of northwest Australia, painted on a rock wall.

People did not necessarily live on their clan country, as bands included members from various clans and wandered over different clan countries. However the clan had to give permission for others to use its country. Of course everyone had certain kinds of relatives in other clans, their mother's, father's mother's or wife's people, and as all the clans in an area were related to one another in this way they could use each other's countries.

The men of each clan were the authorities on the dreamtime events which took place in their own country. They had the right to tell the stories and perform the rituals which drew on the spiritual power deposited in the sacred places in the dreamtime. Many dreamtime people had travelled long distances, passing through the countries of many clans, each of which owned the tales, rituals and sacred places belonging to its own short section of their track. Some of these tracks extended hundreds of miles across Australia, far beyond the knowledge of any single community, into the lands of different tribes speaking different languages. Clans co-operated with their neighbours along the track to perform their rituals. They could travel over one another's land in the steps of the dreamtime people from one sacred site to another. Through these tracks, which linked Aboriginal communities in vast networks across the continent, people could find refuge on each other's land in hard times, and local products could be passed on by trade over vast distances.

Through their relatives and through dreamtime links, communities with their own clan lands and tribal areas could co-operate with one another, and share in the food supply of an area much greater than the one they actually owned. This was especially important to people in the desert areas, where rainfall is very irregular, for when one place dried up and became virtually barren for a while, the local people could rely on the hospitality of more fortunate neighbours.

Men and the dreamtime world

It was the men who became most deeply involved in the dreamtime world. Many sacred tales and rituals belonging to the local clan groups were closely guarded secrets from which women were excluded. Men were only admitted to these secrets after their close kinsmen had put them through elaborate initiation ceremonies. These were often big events in which people from a wide area would gather to initiate their boys or young men all at the same time. The youths were taken away from the company of the womenfolk and young children who would mourn as if they were being taken to their deaths. They might be secluded for several months, during which time their elder kinsmen trained and tested them. When they returned to the camp they were 'reborn' as adult men. They had received their first glimpse of the dreamtime world and of religious responsibilities which women would never share. Not until then were they ready to marry and take on the responsibilities of family life. The training itself was through long-established rituals originating in the dreamtime and varying in different

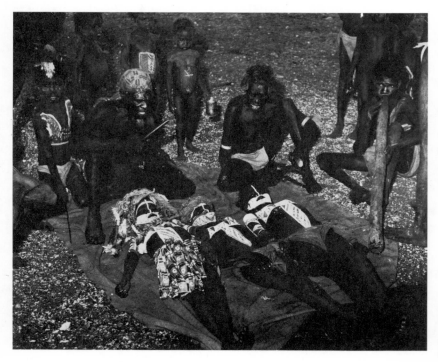

A stage in initiation for boys in Arnhem Land. The boys are painted with special designs and their kinsmen sing to the rhythm of tapping sticks and the drone pipe or 'didjeridu' (1952).

parts of Australia. The youths were tested for physical endurance and the ability to live independently on the land. They also learnt to respect and obey their elders, who had great power over them in these ceremonies, and who tested them for moral worth. These men would consecrate the youths with their own blood, which stood for life and sacred things. The marks of initiation were often left upon the body, for depending on the local custom, the youths would be circumcised, have front teeth knocked out or have decorative scars made on their bodies. These were only some of the painful ordeals all men endured with fortitude to gain admission to the secrets of the dreamtime and of life.

During initiation youths were told about the events of the dreamtime, which their instructors would re-enact for them in other rituals, not necessarily part of the actual initiation rituals. They were shown the sacred places and objects symbolising the dreamtime beings. All these things belonged to the youths because they themselves belonged to the group of people and to its land. The initiated men held these things in trust, disclosing them only if the inheritors were worthy. Men learned more and more about the dreamtime as they grew older, and further ritual secrets were revealed to them. Old men were highly respected for their great knowledge of these matters. Although photos of such secret things have been published in the past, Aborigines today wish to avoid their secrets being revealed in this way. For this reason no secret places or rituals are illustrated in this book.

Of course women had the same spiritual links with the dreamtime as men, but many rituals were never revealed to them. In some areas women had their own secret ritual life, although less elaborate than that of the men. Girls' initiation rituals were simpler and were aimed to prepare them more for marriage and motherhood. If women or uninitiated boys ever stumbled upon the most sacred sites or saw secret objects or rituals belonging to the men they usually had to be killed.

Sacred rituals had to do with events of the dreamtime, which were usually told in songs as part of the ritual. The rituals had various purposes. One was to maintain the state of the world as it should be and always had been, bringing the power of the dreamtime people into the present. The supply of plants and animals, whether food or pests, the weather and other natural forces—all the things in the Aboriginal environment were made to thrive by releasing the 'spirits' of these things from the sacred places where the dreamtime people had left them. The local clans each played their part by bringing their own particular 'totem' creatures or things into being for the benefit of the community as a whole. The rituals for this might be very simple. Sometimes, for instance, the sacred place, a rock or group of stones, only needed to be touched or sprinkled with blood to make the spirits come out and become new creatures. Men used their own blood in many rituals, usually piercing a vein in the arm, for blood was supposed to be the source of life and spiritual strength.

The more elaborate rituals were dramatic re-enactments of dreamtime events, in which men played the parts of the dreamtime people with dancing and singing of the sacred stories. Some of these were originally performed as rituals by the dreamtime people, but all the events of the dreamtime were sacred and these too were acted in rituals.

Initiation rituals were also first performed by the dreamtime people, and men became at one with the dreamtime through their power. In Arnhem Land the most important rituals not only initiated men into the secrets of the dreamtime during their lives, but united their spirits with the dreamtime after their death and burial. Certain dreamtime women and the 'rainbow serpent' originated these rituals, which also ensured the fertility of the plants and creatures, including humans, whose spirits they placed in the sacred sites.

In addition to using these sacred rituals certain men had their own special powers, given to them by spirits of the dead or of the dreamtime. They gained these in mysterious dreams or experiences in which they were specially initiated, perhaps by being killed and brought to life again. These 'medicine-men' had the power to cure illness, to hold seances with spirits and to discover the cause of peoples' deaths. The Aborigines usually explained illness and death as someone working malicious magic, perhaps causing foreign objects to enter the victim's body. Medicine-men could extract these objects and find out who was responsible. In some areas they also had the power to cause illness and death themselves, but there were also ways for ordinary people to do this. Methods included making an image of the victim, or a painting on a rock wall, and inflicting the intended harm upon it, or releasing the spirit of an illness from a place where it was left in the dreamtime. 'Pointing' with a special sharpened bone was supposed magically to pierce the victim at a distance, or to draw his life away. These and many other methods needed training and experience and the use of special chants. Such magic was not always used to harm people; there were similar ways of attracting lovers. However it often seemed to prove effective, much to the surprise of some European observers. Both love affairs and suspected magic were common causes of quarrels and feuds.

Sacred art

An important feature of sacred rituals was the artistic designs which were used to draw on the power of the dreamtime. In all these rituals men taking part had their bodies decorated with sacred designs. These were usually made in coloured bird down or plant fluff stuck on with blood or, especially in Arnhem Land, in paint from clay and ochre earths. These designs symbolised the dreamtime person represented by the actor because they showed the places and events belonging to the dreamtime person. The painting, often with a headdress and other sacred things, transformed men into dreamtime persons. They danced and imitated the behaviour of these beings as if they were actually in the

Dancers in an Arnhem Land ritual covered with down to represent dreamtime people.

dreamtime. Music was provided by singing, usually to the rhythm of sticks or boomerangs tapped together and in northern areas by the drone pipe or 'didjeridu'.

This was only one of the ways dreamtime persons were represented in works of art. In many parts of Australia wooden boards and stone tablets, known as 'tjurunga', were also engraved with sacred designs. These also stood for the journeys of particular dreamtime persons, and thus for these beings themselves. Sometimes the tjurunga was said to be the dreamtime person's body, as rocks and other features of the landscape were. These sacred objects were kept in special 'storehouses' such as crevices in the rocks, at sacred sites from which women and the unitiated were banned. They were brought out only for serious religious purposes. In a ritual they might be made part of a dancer's costume, or be carried by him, or the ritual might be held before the tjurunga, which was specially painted and decorated. Sometimes men merely contemplated the design and tried to absorb the sacred power of the tjurungas by touching them. They would do this to the dancers after a sacred dance. Boards like tjurunga were sometimes used as 'bull-roarers'. When swung around rapidly on the end of a long cord they made an awesome humming, signalling that sacred rituals were taking place.

In central Australia designs like those on the dancers and tjurunga were also painted on a large scale on the ground for rituals. In other parts sculptures were made from the earth. These too showed the dreamtime stories, and like the dancer's decorations they were completely destroyed after use. Sacred paintings or engravings of dreamtime persons were also made on rock walls in some parts of Australia, at sites associated with these beings. These might be permanent symbols of the dreamtime persons, just as tjurunga and sacred sites were.

The exact meaning of the sacred designs is not obvious to anyone seeing them. Shapes might have any number of different meanings depending on the design in which they were used, and they might have several meanings at one time in the same design. The particular dreamtime people and events shown in a design could only be understood once its meaning was explained by someone who knew. The picture

In this simple example the concentric circles could stand for the camp of dreamtime wild-yam people.
This is also the yam root itself, and the hill marking the place where the first yam people emerged from the ground.
The 'U's could be these people sitting around their camp fire and the lines their tracks as they travelled to certain other sacred sites, marked by circles. These tracks also link the Aborigine communities of these places.

(Far left) Repainting the carved posts used in funeral rituals on Melville Island (1962).

(Left) An Arnhem Land man painting a sheet of bark with ochres and clay.

14

shows how several levels of meaning can be combined in one design. By contemplating such designs and having them explained at initiations, Aboriginal men not only learned the sacred stories but came to appreciate some of their deeper religious meanings.

The people of Arnhem Land made sacred objects in a distinctive local style. Wooden sculptures and carved poles and planks were used to represent the dreamtime people. Some of these things were stored away and repainted with bright ochre and clay paints for each ritual. Others, such as carvings of animals, birds, fish and humans were abandoned or destroyed after the ritual. Often they were secret and could only be seen by initiates. Paintings were also done on sheets of tree bark, showing dreamtime characters and events in the same style as on other sacred objects and on ritual dancers. The use of these paintings varied. In some places they were painted as part of the rituals to ensure the supply of plants and wild creatures, in others they were stored in secret and used to explain the dreamtime events they showed to youths at initiation. Today bark paintings are also made for sale to Europeans.

Aborigines in the modern world

Beliefs in the dreamtime show how the Aborigines felt themselves to be truly a part of their environment, and how their lives fitted a pattern which they could see reflected in the world all around them. They believed that the world had remained the same ever since the dreamtime, and they tried to ensure that things continued in this way. They lived according to traditions started by the dreamtime people, and they constantly renewed the spiritual strength of the world in rituals which brought the dreamtime into the present.

This life was inevitably disrupted when Europeans moved into Aboriginal country. There was no room for Aboriginal traditional life and European farming or stockraising on the same land. As the European frontier moved forward in the fertile south during the nineteenth century, Aborigines were often brutally slaughtered as a nuisance to the people who wanted their land. The Aborigines of Tasmania were herded together and kept in virtual captivity until by 1876 they had all died. In the centre and north of Australia European settlement came later, and some Aborigines have managed to retain part of their lands, particularly in Arnhem Land. They have become dependent on European society for food and consumer goods, but their income from employment in stockraising, or doles, does not usually give them a very good living. In fact some areas of the desert supported more people in Aboriginal times than they do by stockraising. Some Aborigines manage to return to the bush for part of the year, living for a short time like their ancestors and holding their sacred rituals. Many have drifted to the cities, where some have managed to adjust to Western life. Others live in slums, alienated from both white and traditional Aboriginal society.

To the conservative, traditional-minded Aborigines the new experiences of a wider world, so different from their own, were a great shock when they first encountered white men. When they also lost the land they loved so dearly, which was the basis of their lives and beliefs, they found it difficult or impossible to continue their old way of life. Their culture was attacked from other sides also, by government authorities and missionaries who wished to change their ways.

The Aborigines have been called savages, 'parasites on nature', stone age survivals and many other unpleasant or condescending things. They were not only thought to be the lowest form of mankind but were treated as subhuman by many of the white people who met them. These ideas continue, in Australia and elsewhere, but serious studies of their way of life have shown things to be very different. Their way of life was indeed vastly different from our own, and lacking in the material possessions, technology and ideas of 'progress' which we value so highly. It was finely adjusted to the environment they lived in, in a way that Western economies cannot achieve. Aborigines lived off the land without destroying or degrading it, or risking the livelihood by over-using their food supply. They treated their environment with the deeply religious reverence which was basic to their whole way of life. How far this way of life can find any place in Australian society remains to be seen.

(Right above) Desert women with digging sticks collecting edible grubs in a wooden bowl (1962).

(Right below) A family from southeastern Australia, on the road to civilisation in the last century.

(Back cover) A man from the northeast coast of Queensland, photographed in the 1890s. He has a painted shield and ceremonial club, and is painted for a ceremony.

Further reading

These books give good general information on Aborigines:

Baglin, D. and Robinson, R., *The Australian Aboriginal in Colour* (A. H. and A. W. Reed, 1968).

Berndt, R. M. and C. H., *The World of the First Australians* (Angus and Robertson, 1964).

Elkin, A. P. *The Australian Aborigines* (Longmans, 1961).

The British Museum also publishes *The Australian Aborigines* by B. A. L. Cranstone, dealing particularly with material culture.

Books may be consulted in the reference library of the Museum of Mankind.

©1977 The Trustees of the British Museum

Published by British Museum Publications Limited, 6 Bedford Square, London WC1B 3RA

Designed by James Shurmer

Illustrations appear by courtesy of the following: Australian Information Service, front cover, pages 13, 14 (right); Museum of Mankind Archives, inside front cover, inside back cover (below), back cover, pages 6, 9; David Attenborough, inside back cover (top), page 14 (left); Axel Poinant, pages 3, 10.

Drawings on pages 4, 14 by Ben Burt

ISBN 0 7141 0060 9

Printed in England by Martin Cadbury, Worcester